Toad plodded down to the pond.   Frog watched her, then jumped out from behind a tree stump.   "Did I make you jump?" said Frog, then added "but you can't jump can you!"

Toad took no notice and started to drink. She could see some fish and little black tadpoles in the clear water.

"Look how well I can jump," shouted Frog, and he jumped over Toad and landed on a lily leaf frightening all the fish.

For a while Frog practised diving into the pond, then he jumped from one waterlily to another.

A large pike swam to the top of the pond and watched Frog.

"Look out!" shouted Toad as the pike jumped out of the water and tried to catch Frog.   Frog made an extra big jump and landed on the bank.

"Did you see his sharp teeth?" asked Frog as he jumped away into some long grass. Toad was pleased to be alone again and she crawled under her favourite log and waited for her supper to come by.

She had just caught a fly and a moth when suddenly the log began to move. Two little hands grabbed Toad and put her into a jam jar. The children took her to the pond and started fishing with their nets.

Toad tried to get out but the sides of the jar were too slippery.
"Help !" cried Toad, but no one could hear her.

She looked up at the blue sky and saw some ducks flying over. "Help!" but they couldn't help her either. But Frog knew she was in the jar. He had been watching the children all the time.

Frog crept up to the jar and pushed his face against the glass. "I'll get you out," he said, but he didn't know how he would do it. He pushed and pushed but the jar would not fall over.

So he went away to think. "Quickly, get me out," called Toad. Frog jumped high in the air.

He landed with a crash on the top of the jar and it fell over. Now Toad could crawl out.   The little boy tried to catch her but she jumped into the pond just in time.

Frog dived in too and together they swam to the other side. "I didn't think you could jump," said Frog.

"I can when I'm frightened," said Toad. "I'll race you home," said Frog who started to jump away as fast as he could. "Thank you for saving me," shouted Toad, but Frog was already too far away to hear.

"Frog is always in a hurry. He misses all the best things," thought Toad as she caught a beetle and a tasty worm.

PHOTOGRAPHY CREDITS: ©Joseph De Leo/Foodpix/Getty Images; 2 (c) ©Gilbert S. Grant/Photo Researchers/Getty Images; 3 (c) ©Joseph De Leo/Foodpix/Getty Images; 4 (c) ©Tony Freeman/Photo Researchers, Inc.; 4 (l) ©Nordic Photos/Superstock; 5 (c) ©Martin Shields/Photo Researchers/Getty Images; 6 (c) ©Bob Gibbons/age fotostock; 7 (c) ©Y and S Creators/age fotostock/Superstock

Copyright © by Houghton Mifflin Harcourt Publishing Company

All rights reserved. No part of this work may be reproduced or transmitted in any form or by any means, electronic or mechanical, including photocopying or recording, or by any information storage and retrieval system, without the prior written permission of the copyright owner unless such copying is expressly permitted by federal copyright law. Requests for permission to make copies of any part of the work should be addressed to Houghton Mifflin Harcourt Publishing Company, Attn: Contracts, Copyrights, and Licensing, 9400 Southpark Center Loop, Orlando, Florida 32819-8647.

Printed in the U.S.A.

ISBN: 978-0-544-07207-7

4 5 6 7 8 9 10 1083 21 20 19 18 17 16

4500608168   A B C D E F G

Inside a Seed!

by Kristen Kunkel

If you have received these materials as examination copies free of charge, Houghton Mifflin Harcourt Publishing Company retains title to the materials and they may not be resold. Resale of examination copies is strictly prohibited.

Possession of this publication in print format does not entitle users to convert this publication, or any portion of it, into electronic format.

adult plant

seedpod with seeds inside

lima bean plant

Plants have a life cycle.
Many plants grow from seeds.
They grow to be adult plants.

lima bean

food

A bean is a seed.
If you open the seedpod, you can see the beans.

The seed coat opens.
It gets light, air, and water.
It has space to grow.

adult plant

flower

The plant keeps growing.
It becomes an adult plant.
It has seedpods with seeds inside.

An Adult Plant

seed pod

The adult plant makes seeds.
The seeds may grow new plants.
The new plants will look like their parent plant.

Responding

Observe a Life Cycle
Plant a fast-growing, flowering plant, such as a marigold. Observe the plant as it changes from a seed to an adult plant. Draw pictures to show the different stages in the plant's life cycle, including seed, seedling, and flower. Have children discuss why a plant looks like its parent plant.

Identify Plant Parts
Look at a picture of a flowering plant in a book or magazine. Use self-stick notes to label the plant's parts. Work with a partner to use resources in your classroom and/or library to learn how the plant uses its parts. Write sentences about what you learned. Ask your teacher for help as needed.

Vocabulary

adult plant	seed coat
air	seedpod
flower	seeds
leaf	soil
life cycle	space to grow
light	sprout
roots	stem